Portraits Album

WELCOME AND THANK YOU! Each page is a portrait, suitable for cut-out and framing. This album is a nice conversation piece in your sala or coffee table. Published by Tatay Jobo Elizes, ISBN 13: 978- 1548092313 & ISBN 10: 1548092312

Tatay Jobo, 1960s

Tatay Jobo, 2010s

Portraits Album

Nanay Cora, 1990s

Nanay Cora, 2010s

Ester (Tetchie) Elizes Bowen

Portraits Album

Ester (Tetchie) Elizes Bowen

Portraits Album

Noelle Marie (Nowie) Elizes Bowen

Portraits Album

Noelle Mari (Nowie) Elizes Bowen

Portraits Album

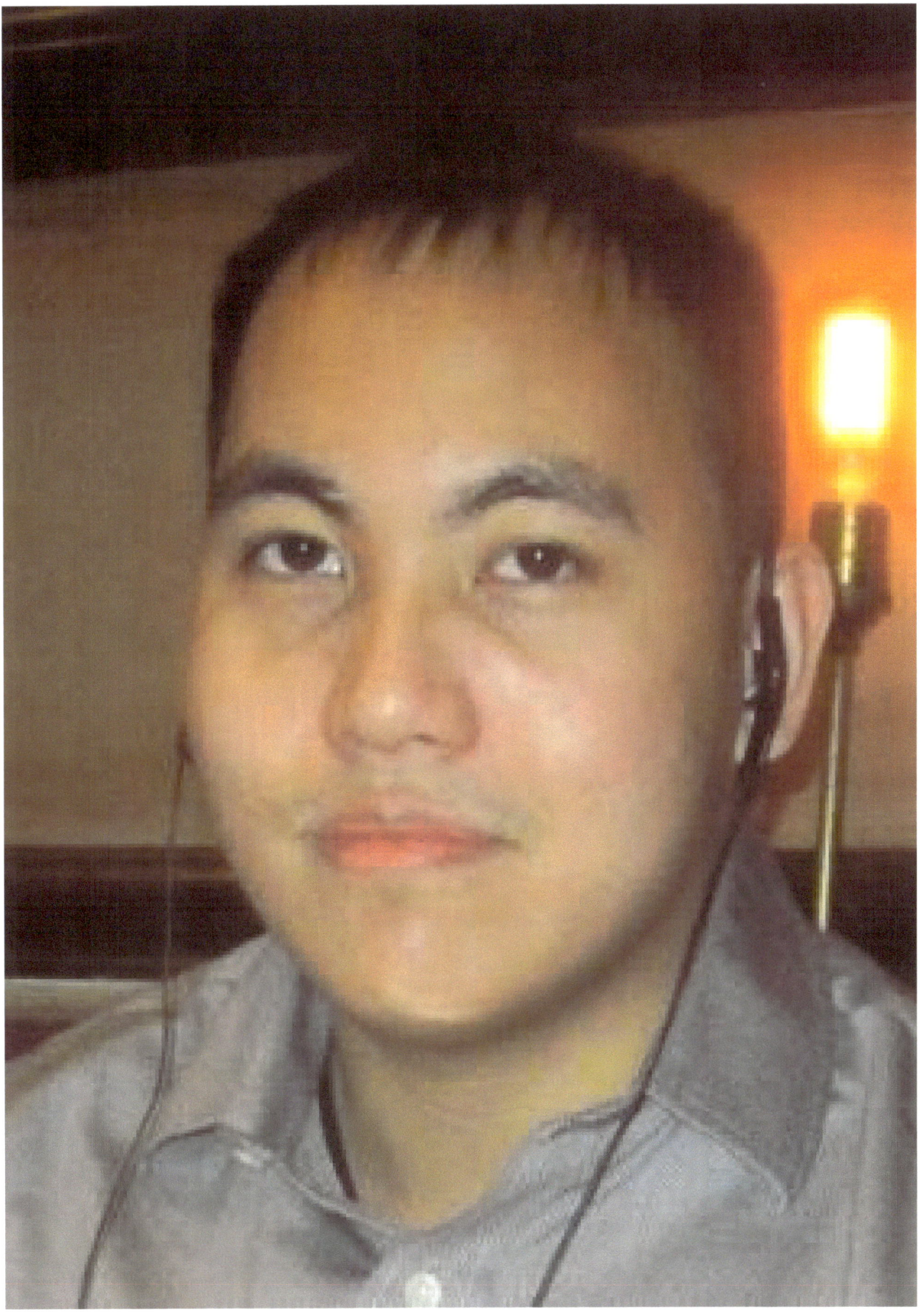

Jeb Elizes

Portraits Album

Jeb Elizes

Portraits Album

Chevalier (Chevy) Elizes

Portraits Album

Chevalier (Chevy) Elizes

Portraits Album

Elizabeth (Abaeth) Elizes

Portraits Album

Elizabeth (Abeth) Elizes

Karines (Karin) Elizes Mra

Portraits Album

Karines (Karin) Elizes Mra

Portraits Album

Karines & Aung Mra

Portraits Album

Aung Mra

Portraits Album

Sons Jason and Carson with parents Karin & Aung Mra

Chad Elizes

Chad Elizes

Christy Reyes

Christy Reyes

Portraits Album

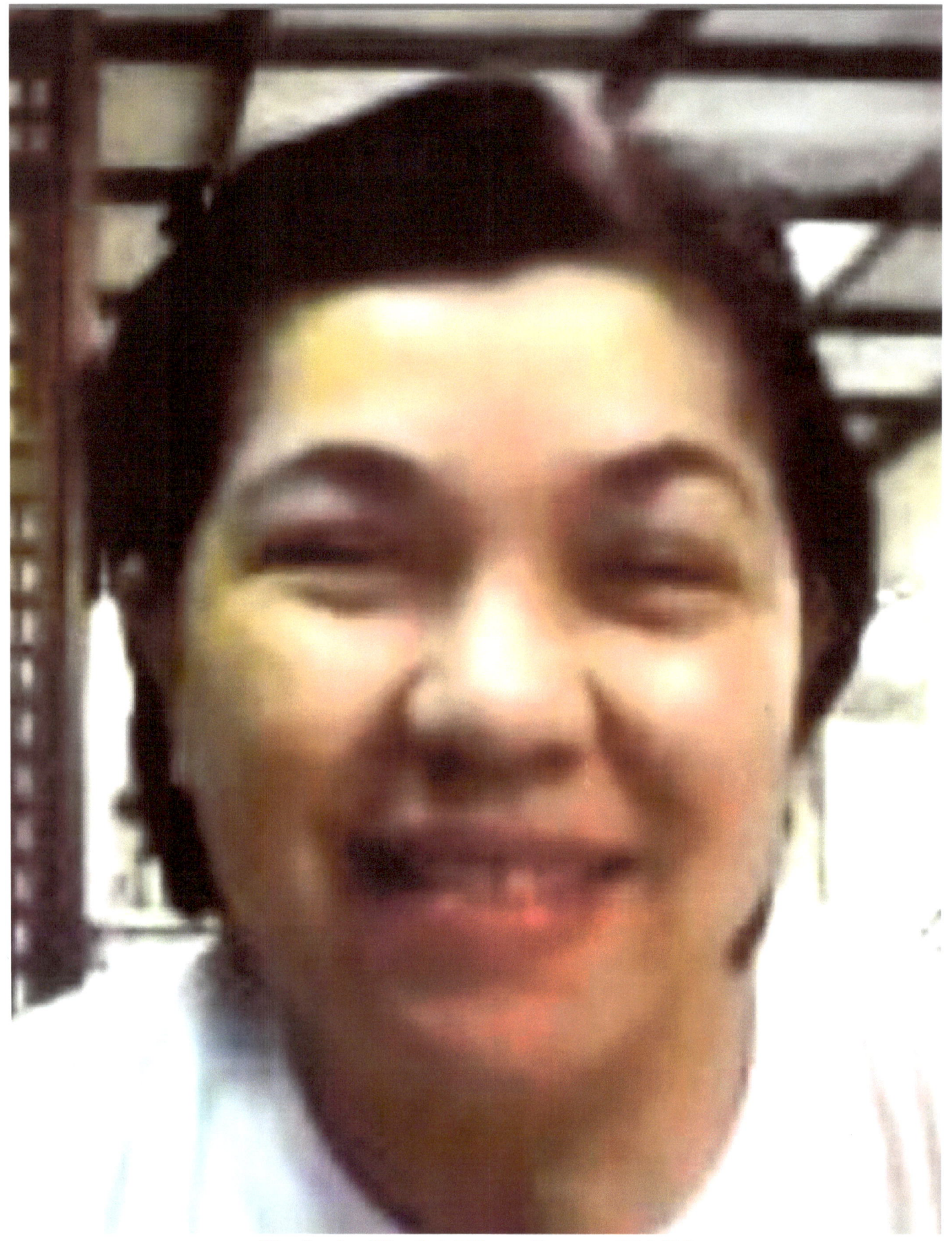

Marinela (Marie) Elizes Reyes. (R.I.P.)

Marinela (Marie) Elizes Reyes, (R.I.P.)

Vincent (Bimbo) Reyes

Vincent (Bimbo) Reyes

Portraits Album

Marjorie Ann (Marjo) Elizes Reyes

Marjorie Ann (Marjo) Elizes Reyes

Portraits Album

Marvin Elizes Reyes

Portraits Album

Marvin Elizes Reyes

Portraits Album

Marty Elizes Reyes

Portraits Album

Marty (Federer) Elizes Reyes

Portraits Album

Grace Esmeralda, Abeth's sister

Portraits Album

Grace Esmeralda, Abeth's sister

Portraits Album

Maydee Esmeralda, Abeth's sister

Portraits Album

Maydee Esmeralda, Abeth's sister

Chiqui Hollman-Yulo, Jobo's cousin

Anita (Annie) Olis Moran, abeth's cousin

Portraits Album

Barry Moran, Anita's husband

Portraits Album

Genalin Esmeralda Soriano, Abeth's niece

www.ingramcontent.com/pod-product-compliance
Lightning Source LLC
Chambersburg PA
CBHW051109180526
45172CB00002B/837